Planning the Perfect Wedding

Planning the Perfect Wedding

Consultant Editor
Antonia van der Meer

A MARSHALL EDITION
CONCEIVED, EDITED AND DESIGNED BY
MARSHALL EDITIONS LTD
THE ORANGERY
161 NEW BOND STREET
London W1Y 9PA

First published in the UK in 1999 by
Marshall Publishing Ltd.

PROJECT EDITOR Tessa Paul
CONSULTANT Antonia van der Meer
EDITOR Jane Laing
DTP EDITOR Lesley Gilbert
ART EDITOR Imran Ghoorbin
PRODUCTION James Bann

TEXT BY
Antonia Cunningham, Sue George, Sarah Halliwell,
Nina Hathway, Tessa Paul

Printed and bound in Italy

Contents

CHAPTER 1
First steps 6

CHAPTER 2
What kind of wedding? 26

CHAPTER 3
What kind of reception? 44

CHAPTER 4
Getting down to details 58

CHAPTER 5
Countdown to the big day 88

CHAPTER 6
Checklists 102
Legal and religious requirements 112

1

First steps

❧

CONGRATULATIONS! You are getting married. And from now until your wedding day you will have an enormous amount of organising to do.

The first thing you have to do is to announce your engagement. The first people to tell will be your parents and your fiancé's parents. It is no longer necessary for the groom to ask the bride's father for his permission to marry her – although many do so as a mark of respect – but you will want both sets of parents on your side. Once you have told them, you are officially engaged.

Many couples also choose to hold a party to celebrate their engagement with their close friends and family. Traditionally, the engagement is formally announced during the evening, and a toast is offered to the couple. And this is the perfect time to show off your engagement ring in public.

Formal announcements

You may also want to insert an announcement in the local or national press. This is a good way of letting neighbours and acquaintances know that you are getting married. It is customary for the bride's parents place the announcement – unless the couple are not very young or are marrying for a second time.

The usual form of wording for a newspaper announcement is as follows:

Mr Nigel Norris and Miss Melanie Mayhew
The engagement has been announced between Nigel, only son of Mr and Mrs John Norris of Acre Lane, Wimbledon, and Melanie, youngest daughter of Mr and Mrs Brian Mayhew of Browngate Manor, Preston, Lancashire.

An alternative wording is as follows:
The marriage has been announced (and will shortly take place) between Nigel...

If your or your fiancé's parents are divorced, separated, widowed or re-married, then the wording of the announcement is more complicated. So, if your father is dead and your mother has remarried, the wording would be: "daughter of the late Mr Brian Mayhew and Mrs James Morrison". If your father is dead and your mother has not remarried, it would be: "Melanie, youngest daughter of the late Mr Brian Mayhew and Mrs Mayhew". If your parents are divorced and your mother has not remarried, the wording would be: "daughter of Mr Brian Mayhew and Mrs Jane Mayhew".

Newspapers usually have a form to complete for such announcements, and completing one will ensure you avoid embarrassing spelling mistakes. Make sure you or your parents tell your families when the announcement will be appearing in the paper so that they can buy a copy.

Choosing the ring

EVEN THOUGH IT'S NOT essential to have an engagement ring, most women want to wear one. It's a way of showing the world that you're going to be married.

Traditionally, an engagement ring is bought by the groom who presents it to the bride as part of a proposal of marriage. These days, however, couples usually choose an engagement ring together, and the groom pays for it. As a guideline, the ring should cost no more than about a month of the groom's salary. There is a huge range of styles and prices available and it is worth shopping around for something you really like. Diamonds and other precious stones can be cut with a number of different facets or sides. The more facets a stone has, the more brightly it sparkles. This is known as the cut.

When choosing an engagement ring, it is worth considering the sort of wedding ring you will be wearing, as some engagement rings can get in the way of wedding bands. You might like to choose both at the same time or buy one of the many matching wedding and engagement ring sets available.

Antique rings can be an unusual option, although they are often very expensive. In some families, rings are passed down through the generations. With such rings, it is essential that the ring is sized to fit properly – a professional jeweller will be able to do this. Make sure, too, that the ring is valued and insured.

Even though it is not legally essential, the giving of a wedding ring – gold, white gold or platinum, depending on your budget – is a central part of the wedding ceremony. Give careful consideration to the sort of ring that will suit you, as you will be wearing it permanently. These days many men also choose to wear a ring, and matching rings are available in many styles.

Birthstones

Choosing your birthstone for your engagement ring is a very popular option, and wearing your fiancé's birthstone is said to bring particularly good luck.

Aries	*(March 21-April 20)*	Aquamarine
Taurus	*(April 21-May 20)*	Diamond
Gemini	*(May 21-June 20)*	Emerald
Cancer	*(June 21-July 20)*	Pearl
Leo	*(July 21-August 21)*	Ruby
Virgo	*(August 22-Sept 22)*	Peridot
Libra	*(September 23-October 22)*	Sapphire
Scorpio	*(October 23-Nov 22)*	Opal
Sagittarius	*(November 23-Dec 20)*	Topaz
Capricorn	*(December 21-Jan 19)*	Turquoise
Aquarius	*(January 20-February 19)*	Garnet
Pisces	*(February 20-March 20)*	Amethyst

Legal matters

I N ENGLAND AND WALES, you can marry in one of three different places: a church (or other place of worship, such as a synagogue or mosque); a registry office; or other specially approved premises. There are a few legal requirements to fulfil wherever you are going to be married. The marriage must be held in public before two adult witnesses. The bride and groom must both be over 16 and, if either is under 18, it is essential that they have the permission of their legal guardians. Neither party may still be married to anyone else. The marriage must be conducted by an authorised person – a registrar or a minister.

Marrying in church

Many couples want to marry in church. This may be because of a sincerely held faith or because they find it more romantic or atmospheric. If you are not a regular church-goer but wish to marry in church, the minister will want to discuss with you your reasons for your choice. Whatever the case, you will be expected to attend pre-wedding classes.

Traditionally, couples marry in the bride's church, and she must have been resident in that district for fifteen days before the ceremony. The banns – notification of the intent of the couple to marry – must be read out by the minister for three Sundays prior to the wedding.

Civil ceremonies

If you do not wish to marry in a church (or other religious premises) you will make other arrangements with the registrar at least three weeks in advance. If you and your partner live in different districts, you must notify both registrars and sign a declaration that there is no legal objection to the marriage. You will then usually marry in a registry office, although you might prefer to choose from a variety of licensed venues, such as stately homes, hotels or even football clubs. The ceremonies carried out in such places are similar to those held in registry offices, but you can add non-religious music or readings if you wish.

Many couples choose to be married abroad and some holiday companies specialise in complete wedding and honeymoon packages. Most countries have some kind of residency requirement – be sure to check.

In Scotland, you can have a religious ceremony anywhere you choose as long as you can persuade the minister. Civil ceremonies can only take place in a registry office. You must give at least two weeks' notice to the registrar in the area you are to be married.

If marrying in a registry office, many couples also like to have an additional personal ceremony in which they can choose their own words and music. Because this is simply a ceremony of commitment rather than a legal requirement, it can be held anywhere.

Second marriages

IT IS BECOMING EVER more common for people to divorce and then remarry. But having a second wedding ceremony is never exactly like the first one and not simply because you are older and wiser.

Traditionally, second marriages are smaller and more informal than the first, although, of course, it is acceptable to have a grand celebration. The couple usually act as hosts and not the bride's parents.

In England and Wales most ministers of the Church of England cannot marry a person who is divorced and whose partner is still living. They will, however, give a blessing to your wedding, following a civil ceremony. During the blessing the couple publicly confirm the promises they have made at the registry office. If you are widowed, of course, there is no such problem.

In Scotland, ministers are often more willing to marry divorcees. However, you will need to discuss matters with your own minister to make sure he is happy to do this.

If you or your fiancé have children from a previous relationship, then you will probably want to give them a central role in the ceremony. After all, they are marrying into a new family, too. Depending on their age, they could act as bridesmaids, attendants, or even give you away.

Prenuptial contracts

In Britain, unlike some other parts of the world, prenuptial contracts are not legally binding. In the event of a marriage breakdown, particularly when children are involved, the courts would consider both partner's needs at that particular time, as well as what each had contributed to the marriage in terms of time and commitment.

Many couples shy away from making prenuptial contracts because they consider that it starts off the marriage on the wrong basis – implying that the marriage will end at some point and that they fundamentally distrust one another.

You might like to consider a very different form of prenuptial contract. Thecouple set out in writing exactly what they are and are not going to do for each other. For example, you may agree not to shout at your husband when he forgets to do the washing up. And he may agree to bring you flowers every Friday. Unfortunately, these prenuptial contracts are also not legally binding!

Setting the date

HAVING ANNOUNCED your intention to marry, you will now need to decide – in conjunction with the groom and both your families – when you are going to get married and what sort of wedding you are going to have.

Is it going to be a lavish church wedding? A quick registry office visit followed by a small dinner party? A quiet wedding abroad? In your home town or where you live now? Will you be marrying in the summer or the winter? How many guests do you want to invite? Are you going to marry on a Saturday or another day of the week?

Allow enough time

Once you have decided what sort of wedding you want, you are in a position to set the date. This is not simply a matter of working out when you as a couple want to marry. You have to figure out when your parents, your closest friends, and the best man and chief bridesmaid will be free. And if you have any friends from abroad who might attend, you have to establish whether they will be able to make it on that particular day.

In addition, when setting the date make sure you give yourself enough time to organise everything for the wedding. Allow at least six months to do this, more if possible. If you are marrying on a popular Saturday in the summer, then the sooner everything is organised the better. Churches, photographers and venues will need to be booked as soon as possible.

If you are having a cake made for you, bakers can require up to eight months' notice; a dress will take four to six months to be made; reception venues and caterers also need six months' notice.

Plan ahead

As a rough guide, six months ahead you should: decide on the number of guests; draft the budget; book the registry office or church; arrange for the banns or licence; book the reception venue; arrange the entertainment; order the cake; select the attendants; book the photographer; arrange the transport; and plan the honeymoon.

Four months ahead you should: order your wedding dress; discuss the bridesmaids' dresses; order the stationery; decide on the menu; order the flowers; discuss the groom's and best man's outfits. Post invitations three months before the wedding date.

Two months ahead you should: organise your wedding hairdressing and make-up; choose the wedding rings; check the church/registry office arrangements; arrange insurance; check guests' accommodation and transport.

One month ahead you should: confirm the reception is progressing smoothly; make sure your dress is nearly ready; give final guest numbers to the venue or caterers.

Bearing the cost

TRADITIONALLY, MOST of the costs of paying for the wedding fall with the bride's family. Nowadays, however, when both men and women work, and when young couples can earn as much as their parents, the considerable expense of a wedding is often shared between the bride, groom and their respective families.

On the other hand it can still be a point of pride to the bride's father that he pay for the wedding. Indeed, often parents anticipate paying for their daughters' weddings, and save for them accordingly. Above all, it is important not to make assumptions about who will pay for what: one or two tactful conversations should find out what both families expect. The groom's family may want to offer to pay for one major item of the wedding expenses, such as the alcohol. Any offers to share costs by the groom's family or yourself or your fiancé should be conducted with the utmost sensitivity: you do not want embarrassment or arguments to mar the planning of your wedding.

Sometimes other people – such as godparents – also want to contribute financially. In such cases it is often a good idea to ask them to pay for one of the larger or more expensive wedding presents rather than contribute to the costs of the wedding itself. After all, you and your new husband will soon have all the financial responsibility that married life entails.

The bride's family pays for:
The reception; bride's outfit; photographer; cars; church and reception flowers; music; stationery.

The groom pays for:
His outfit; church fees; the rings; gifts for wedding party; flowers for the bride and attendants; the honeymoon expenses.

The bridesmaids or attendants and their families may pay for their own outfits – or you do so.

Insurance

Wedding insurance is essential and should cover as much of the expenditure as possible. Otherwise you will be liable for all the costs should something happen to cause your wedding to be cancelled. Some companies specialise in providing this kind of insurance.

A good insurance policy should provide cover against the wedding not happening at all because of the death, illness, accident or redundancy of either you, the groom or close members of your families. It should also cover specific problems such as the reception venue cancelling, a guest being injured and you being held responsible, and the failure of wedding photographs to come out.

Separate policies should be taken out to cover the engagement and wedding rings and travel insurance for the honeymoon.

Budgeting matters

E VERY BRIDE WOULD LIKE to have a limitless amount to spend on her wedding and honeymoon, but unfortunately most people have to be realistic and operate within a budget. This means working out how much they can afford to spend, deciding on exactly what to spend it and then sticking to their decisions as the planning proceeds.

First of all you, your groom and your families will have to decide how much you have available to spend. It is essential that you work out what your overall budget is, and then stick to it. When you work out how much you have to spend, don't forget the many costs you will have to cover afterwards as you set up home.

Prioritise and list everything

Decide on the items you wish to prioritise – those on which you are happy to spend the most money – and make sure that you agree these priorities with the groom! The higher on the list of priorities an item is, the less likely you will be to want to economise on it. For example, for many brides, the most important item will be their wedding dress. And while you may not be willing to cut costs on your dress, you may not mind economising on transport. When you have decided how much your priority items will cost, you will be able to work out how much you have to spend on everything else.

Next, compile a list of everything you can think of which you may need to spend money on. Arrange your list under headings, such as clothing, transport, reception venue, flowers, catering, drinks, entertainment, rings, photography and honeymoon. Then you can see at a glance all the individual items within each category.

You will now need to obtain quotations for as many of your listed items as possible, to get an idea of what is feasible within the budget you have decided upon.

Take note of hidden costs. For example, hire of a reception room may not include hire of glassware and crockery. It is essential that you find out exactly what is included in a quote so that you can compare like with like.

Finalise the details

Having a budget sheet or special computer program for wedding costs can help you to see how the costs are mounting up. Write down every estimate or quotation next to the appropriate item as you receive it. Make sure that you include a contingency sum of five to ten per cent of the total cost of the wedding. There are always a few costs that cannot be foreseen.

When you have worked out the price of every aspect of your wedding, and decided exactly how much you want to spend on what, then you are ready to confirm in writing and send deposits to those companies whose services you have decided to use.

Economy measures

THERE ARE MANY WAYS you can cut the cost of your wedding – and some will hurt more than others. But if you plan sensibly, you can economise and no one – not even you – will notice the difference. With a little imagination, you can have a wedding that is even more memorable than one with a huge budget.

Money-saving tips

Clothing: buy or hire a second-hand wedding dress and other outfits but check the expense of the alterations required to make the clothes fit properly, and of the dry-cleaning costs on hired items; wear flowers in your hair instead of a headdress; shop in the sales; find out whether you can borrow any items of your wedding outfit.

Reception: shorten your guest list. You don't really need to invite all those people you haven't seen for years; invite a few guests to a sit-down meal and a larger number to an evening party; if marrying on approved premises, have your reception and first night of your honeymoon there; serve sparkling wine or bucks fizz instead of champagne; buy the drinks yourself; consider having the reception in a private house; ask friends or relatives to put up wedding guests; decorate the venue with balloons and streamers rather than fresh flowers; choose an inexpensive place for the reception (such as a village or church hall) and make it romantic by adding bowls of floating candles and draped muslin to camouflage bare walls.

Photography: people often economise by taking the photographs or videos themselves, or getting their friends to do it (*see pages 72–73*).

Transport: walk to the reception; use your own car – perhaps decorating it yourself too; hire an ordinary taxi.

Other: design and make your own wedding stationery – many simple-to-use computer programs are available; use flowers from your own and friends' gardens for decoration and your bouquet; carry a single bloom instead of a bouquet.

Exercise caution

Close friends and relatives can often help out by catering, bar-tending and so on. For your own peace of mind, however, you must have absolute trust in the ability of the person to do what they are offering. If you are not totally certain that Auntie Maud can make your wedding cake, then you should not take up her offer.

Many brides, or their relatives, want to tackle the challenge of making a wedding dress themselves. But unless they are professional dressmakers, they should beware. Wedding dresses are tremendously difficult and complicated to make. The fabric is expensive, and if it all goes wrong, you will have wasted your money and given yourself a whole lot more stress.

Creating your wedding team

IT MAY BE YOUR WEDDING but it takes a real team effort to make it successful. And in getting your team together, you will need to consider carefully who will be best for each role, and to exercise masses of diplomacy.

Allocate roles carefully

On your wedding day, you will want to be surrounded and helped by those closest to you; both the bride and groom's family and friends should be included as your attendants. Problems may arise when one person is asked rather than another. If you have more potential adult attendants than you need, it may be worth getting them together to explain your problem. Some will perhaps prefer not to undertake the role you have in mind, while others may have demanding work or family responsibilities that mean they simply do not have the time.

When it comes to choosing a chief bridesmaid, maid of honour or best man, you need someone responsible and sensible, who will be able to keep calm throughout and especially when you are panicking. You need them to help with invitations, shopping, thank you cards and to take care of gifts and clothes after the wedding.

Small children, particularly little girls, are often very keen to be involved in the wedding ceremony, but you will not be able to have an endless number of flower girls on the day. Consult with their parents: perhaps inviting only the eldest children may be a solution. To make the smaller ones feel part of your wedding, you might give them a gift on the day.

Some issues can be decidedly tricky. A bride with a much-loved father and stepfather, for instance, will want to include both of them in her wedding. Perhaps one could walk you down the aisle and the other give the wedding speech at the reception.

Consult both families

Most importantly, you need to be able to get what you want without alienating those closest to you. It is an excellent start for your married life if you and your fiancé are able to make joint decisions in the planning of the wedding. When it comes to the rest of your family, however, you may find that their ideas as to how the marriage should be celebrated are not identical with yours.

Generally speaking, the more money your parents have spent on the wedding, the more they will want a say in the running of the event. One area of potential conflict is the guest list. Perhaps you and the groom want to invite all your friends, but both sets of parents believe that inviting family members is more important than inviting friends. In this and many other cases you will just have to work out a compromise.

Planning your honeymoon

I N YEARS GONE BY the honeymoon was the first oppor-
tunity a couple had to spend time together. The bride
had often not travelled at all, and if she had, she would
have been very heavily chaperoned. The honeymoon was
the first chance she had to act as an adult woman.

Nowadays, however, both bride and groom have usually spent a great deal of time alone together, and know
each other well. Nevertheless, they still want to have a
special, romantic holiday. Sometimes this can get out of
hand, as their desire for a "holiday of a lifetime" becomes
the need to spend two weeks in unheard-of luxury.

Decide what you both want

A honeymoon should be one of the most memorable
holidays of your life. Yet with all the other aspects of your
wedding to organise, it can be hard to give it the attention
it deserves. With a little forethought and planning, however, you should be set for an exciting and relaxing time.

First of all, you need to figure out what sort of honeymoon you want. Look in as many holiday brochures as
possible. Some holiday companies specialise in honey-

moon packages; others offer honeymooners certain extras, such as four-poster beds, honeymoon suites, champagne in the room. Then, having gained a rough idea of how much the sort of honeymoon you would like may cost, you will be able to set yourself a realistic budget.

What sort of holiday would suit you? Traditionally, honeymooning couples spent two weeks away from their family and friends. While many couples do still yearn for this kind of splendid isolation, others would rather choose a honeymoon that involves a shared interest, such as scuba-diving, skiing or touring the galleries in a city that they have never visited before.

Whatever you decide, it can be worth arranging to have your wedding night at a hotel near the reception venue. After an exhausting and exciting day, you will probably not want to spend hours travelling. But if you are able to depart at a civilised hour after a good night's sleep you will be ready for the honeymoon journey.

Honeymoon options

What's your preferred honeymoon destination? Do you like holidays built around a particular activity or interest? Do you want to relax on the beach? Is a sightseeing holiday more your style? Do you want to travel far? Do you crave quiet and seclusion or would you prefer to holiday in a place where other people honeymoon?

2

What kind of wedding?

❧❧❧

G ETTING MARRIED IS A very exciting and emotional event and it is important that you and the groom feel comfortable with the way in which you publicly declare your love and intention to make a life together.

Religious or civil ceremony?

In choosing the kind of wedding you would like, the first question to consider is whether you would prefer a civil marriage or a religious one. This can be a difficult question to resolve if you belong to a different faiths or denominations, or one of you does not have any religious beliefs. Whatever you decide, make sure that you discuss the matter fully and that you are both content with the decision that you have made. If one, or both of you, are divorced, you may be married in church at the discretion of the religious officer leading the service, except in the Catholic church where it is strictly forbidden. If you cannot be married in church, you may be allowed a blessing ceremony in church at a later date.

For a religious ceremony, you may choose to marry at a place of worship that you know and like, which has family associations or where you know the minister very well. However, if for some reason, your local place of worship does not fit the bill – you dislike the building, it is not convenient for many of your guests or any other reason – you will have to consider other places and organise the administration accordingly. Be prepared for this to take a while.

If you decide on a civil wedding, these can take place in a registry office, or, in England and Wales, in an "approved" building. Lists of these can be bought from the Office of National Statistics and you will probably be able to hold the reception at the same venue if you want to. Civil weddings can be made as personal or as formal as you wish (*see pages 28–29*).

Formal or informal celebration?

Be very clear as to the sort of ceremony and celebration that you would like and where you would like to hold it. Receptions can take place anywhere – at home, at your favourite pub or restaurant, at a nearby stately home, sports club, church hall – anywhere, in fact, that will hire or lend you the right space on the right day.

Do you want a small, intimate wedding, a large, formal one, or something in between? What about flowers and candles, stand-up buffet or sit-down meal, number of speeches? You must discuss all these things with your fiancé and your families, if they are involved in the planning. Take care to organise a wedding and reception that is exactly what you want and which you can afford – for you are not planning on having another one.

Civil weddings

CIVIL WEDDINGS last up to half an hour and can take place between 8 a.m. and 6 p.m., Monday to Friday, and in some places on Saturdays. They take place in a registry office, or, in England and Wales, you may choose an approved, or licensed, building (*see page 27*), which range from stately homes to football clubs, zoos to permanently-moored boats. However, you cannot choose to have your wedding outdoors, inside a marquee or in a private home. In England and Wales, parental consent is required if you are under 18, or under 16 in Scotland.

The purpose of a civil wedding is to legally bind a couple in the eyes of the state. In a registry office, the guests assemble in a waiting room about 15 minutes in advance and the bridal party arrives shortly afterwards. Everyone enters the office, the proceedings are explained and the wedding fees paid. The couple then declare that there is no reason why they should not be joined lawfully in matrimony – neither is already married for example – and call upon the people present to witness the marriage. The couple, two witnesses and the Superintendant and the Registrar then sign the register. An exchange of rings is optional. Note that registry offices are often small, so you should ask how many guests you can invite.

Although civil weddings in a registry office tend to be shorter and more functional than religious weddings, it is possible to introduce readings and music (of a secular nature) if you arrange it with your registrar in advance. The bride may also wear traditional clothing and be given away by her father if she wishes. The only constraint on introducing other elements to the ceremony is time – in a registry office, another wedding party is probably waiting.

A civil wedding in an approved building can be more leisurely, but the fees will be higher because they include the full cost of the Superintendant and Registrar attending. If you would like some sort of ritual or ceremony that solemnizes your wedding for you on a spiritual and personal level, this can be arranged after the civil ceremony has taken place. It can take place anywhere, indoors or out, and include secular and religious elements.

Preparations

You must notify the local Superintendant Registrar of the wedding and make a provisional booking at the registry office up to 12 months, and not less than 17 days (15 days in Scotland), in advance, depending on whether you will be married by Licence or Certificate. To apply for a Licence in England and Wales, one of you must have a 15-day residential qualification and the wedding may take place on the 17th day. A Certificate requires both partners to have lived in the area for seven days and 21 days' notice of the wedding must be given. In Scotland there is no residential requirement. The notice to marry lasts up to 12 months.

Religious ceremonies

Christian weddings

ALL CHRISTIAN DENOMINATIONS, apart from the Christian scientists, can hold weddings in their own churches. As soon as possible get in touch with the church where you wish to get married, as they are usually booked up well in advance. If you and your fiancé are of different denominations, you may be able to arrange for both ministers to attend at the service.

Most priests or ministers will expect you to come to worship at least a few times before you get married and you will be required to discuss the expectations and meaning of marriage with them beforehand. If the parish runs marriage classes, you may be asked to attend.

Most Christian services are similar and the Anglican service is the most widespread. The groom and the guests gather in church before the bride arrives. She comes down the aisle, to music, usually on her father's arm and often followed by bridesmaids or pageboys. She meets the groom, who is standing with his "best man" at the altar. The clergyman welcomes the congregation, discusses the purpose of marriage and asks the couple if there is any reason why they should not be married. The wedding vows follow in which the couple promise themselves to each other "for better, for worse, for richer, for poorer, in sickness and in health, to love and to cherish, till death us do part". The groom gives his bride a ring and she may also give him one. A sermon, hymns, music and, on occasion, the Holy Communion service, are followed by the signing of the civil register. The bride and groom depart down the aisle, as music plays, followed by their attendants and family. Everyone else follows after.

Quaker weddings

Quaker weddings are the least formal of the Christian services and usually take place at the Meeting House, although they can take place anywhere, including in a private home. Clothing is plain, and there is no ceremonial or music. The couple declare their feelings for each other in their own words when they feel ready, in front of the congregation. Anyone who wishes to stand up and speak may do so. The civil register is signed and witnessed. Rings may be exchanged but are not considered a necessary part of the proceedings.

Roman Catholic weddings

If both bride and groom are Catholic, the Roman Catholic service will usually be part of a Nuptial Mass. In order to be married in a Catholic church, non-Catholics marrying Catholics will usually have to show a willingness to allow any children to be brought up Catholic.

Jewish weddings

Jewish marriages are exempt from the usual legal times and places and can be celebrated outdoors, although they usually take place in the synagogue. They never take place on the Sabbath (Saturday) or on certain festivals. Orthodox Jews spend the day before the wedding in prayer and the bride goes to the *mikveh*, a ritual bath. Jewish weddings are performed by a rabbi in the presence of a quorum of ten Jewish men.

The bride, her veil up, waits in a room outside the synagogue. The groom, and his attendants, some carrying candles, lowers the veil. He is then led to the synagogue by the bride's father. He waits beneath the *chuppah*, the canopy under which the marriage is celebrated, while the choir sings blessings on the couple. The bride, led by her mother or mother-in-law, joins the groom. In some ceremonies, she walks around him seven times. Blessings are sung and the couple drink from the marriage cup, the wedding is blessed and the groom "consecrates" himself to the bride with a ring. In Reform ceremonies, the bride does the same. The *Ketubah*, the marriage vows, are read by the rabbi and he, or the guests, recite the Seven Benedictions. The groom crushes a glass symbolically beneath his feet and the guests shout "Mazel tov" (good luck) to the couple.

Celebrations are a joyous affair, with singing and dancing. Orthodox festivities last a week, with parties and the couple "at home" to their friends and family.

Hindu weddings

Hindu weddings are large, family affairs and traditionally take place at the bride's home, although they may take place in a Marriage Hall. The bride, usually dressed in a red (but sometimes green) and gold sari, arrives first, brought by her mother's brother and her family. The groom, in white, arrives later with his family. There are two priests, one for the bride and one for the groom, and a ceremonial fire is lit in the room.

The couple face each other, separated by a curtain, sacred texts are read and the couple are declared to be married. The curtain is removed, musicians play and the bride and groom exchange flower garlands. They are showered with rice, flowers and blessings. Sweets are then distributed among the guests. Popped rice is thrown into the fire and the couple walk around it seven times. Food and celebrations follow.

Muslim weddings

The Muslim marriage ceremony varies depending on the place or country where the celebration takes place. There is no fixed service but, like weddings everywhere, the festivities are often lavish.

The wedding ceremony usually takes place in a hall or the bride's own home. The couple arrive separately – the groom with the men and the bride with the women – and sit in different rooms. The bride may be dressed in traditional embroidered clothing. They are each asked by the *Imam,* or whoever is overseeing the vows – it can be anybody who understands the religious aspects of marriage – if they consent to the union. The groom is asked if he can meet the dowry the bride's family expect for their daughter. At some weddings, he will recite verses from the *Qu'ran,* the Islamic holy scripture. Everybody asks God to bless the marriage, then the bride and groom are allowed to meet. Among some Muslims, the bridal couple sit on a raised dais where they can be viewed by all their guests during the post-wedding celebrations. Among others, the men and women enjoy the festivities in separate rooms.

Sikh weddings

Sikh ceremonies follow similar customs to the Hindu and Muslim ceremonies. The wedding takes place at the *gurdwara*, the Sikh temple, or in the bride's home, and involves hymns, prayers and readings from the *Guru Granth Sahib*, the holy book. The bride wears a red sari or *shalwar-kameez* and a veil that is lifted once she is married. She wears gold jewellery given by the groom's family. The groom may wear traditional white or Western clothing. Parties are held and gifts exchanged.

Buddhist weddings

Marriage has no religious significance for any Buddhist sect and Buddhist weddings that take place in other countries, such as China, India and Japan, usually follow local wedding customs. In the UK, after a civil marriage, a ceremony might take place that involves the exchange of white scarves – symbols of love and spiritual light – and the "exchange of cups", which is a Japanese Buddhist custom.

Unusual venues

SINCE 1994, COUPLES can marry just about anywhere they like, as any building open to the public in
England and Wales can apply for a wedding licence.
People get married at stately homes, castles, football clubs,
racecourses, pubs, boats and even zoos. There are some
places you cannot get married, however, such as in a private home or on a moving vehicle.

The honeymoon wedding

Getting married abroad is an option, and many couples
now choose a Caribbean wedding – Mauritius, the
Seychelles and Bali are also popular spots. You can arrange
for the ceremony to happen on the beach, and have your
wedding party dressed in beach clothes. These tropical
island venues also offer lush, beautiful gardens and warm,
balmy nights which all extend your options for a truly
unusual ceremony. Las Vegas is another popular destination, where couples enjoy kitsch wedding chapels and
being serenaded by Elvis impersonators. It can cost a lot
less to get married abroad, and you can always have a
party or blessing when you return home.

Why not combine your wedding and your honeymoon
into one beautiful package by inviting close family and
friends along with you to the vacation spot of your dreams
and then holding the wedding ceremony there?

A honeymoon (or destination) wedding takes place over the course of a few days in an inviting setting full of amusing and relaxing things to do. The wedding itself can be as formal or informal as you wish, as elaborate or as simple as one you might have had elsewhere. Guests are usually responsible for their own lodging and transportation but you provide most of the food and perhaps pay for some of the activities.

To plan a honeymoon wedding, begin your arrangements at least a year in advance. Contact tourist boards and travel agencies for details of all-inclusive wedding packages and investigate legal requirements for marriage demanded in the country you have chosen. There are hotels at favoured destinations that will help you make all the necessary arrangements for your wedding, or the hotel will give you the name of a consultant in the area who can arrange for the cermony site, officiant, flowers, photography, music and more.

Most important of all, make sure the marriage cermony is legally binding in Britain. If it is not, but you still want to combine your wedding with your honeymoon, organise a civil ceremony in Britain but have a romantic service of blessing at the holiday destination.

Ultimately it's your day, and you can choose the most romantic wedding you can afford. Whether it's in New York's Central Park or on an Italian hillside or in a perfect tropical paradise; in a stately home, romantic hotel or castle, make your wedding day an occasion that you enjoy and one that is very special to you and your guests.

Readings

R EADINGS AT WEDDINGS are very personal and need to be chosen with care. In religious ceremonies, it is customary to choose passages from the Bible and your minister or religious leader will usually help you make your choice.

In Christian services, there are usually two readings, one of which, at least, will come from the Bible. Apart from any help your minister or priest will give you, there are several books available that will present you with a wide choice. Otherwise, you can use a Lectionary to discover a range of passages that relate to love, marriage and children. Here you are bound to find some verses or poems that express your sentiments.

At civil ceremonies it is illegal to have readings with any religious content or reference to God. However, once the registrar has left, or you have moved into another room or venue, you may use whatever readings you like – religious or secular – as part of a private ceremony before your friends and family.

Secular readings

In addition to readings from the Bible, there are plenty of secular readings and poems that can be used to express what you feel for each other, what you mean by your com-

Suitable Bible readings include

Old Testament
Genesis: 1:26-7.31; 2:18-14; 21:48-41; 21:58-67
Song of Solomon: 2:8-10.14.16; 8:6-7
Book of Jeremiah: 31:31-34

Tobit 7:8-15; 8:4-8

New Testament
Romans: 8:31-35. 37-39; 12:1-2.9-18 or 12:1-2.9-13
I Corinthians: 13:1-13
Ephesians: 5:2.21-33 or 5:2.25-32
Colossians: 3:12-17

First letter of St Peter: 3:1-9
First letter of St John: 3:18-24; 4:7-12

mitment and the hopes that you have for the future. You may even like to write a piece yourself, or ask a friend to do so. There are many anthologies of love poetry available and even some that have been chosen specifically with the theme of marriage in mind.

If you are having a religious ceremony but would like one of your readings to be a poem or a prose extract, discuss the possibility of using it with your minister or priest, and you may be able to incorporate it into the service. The minister or priest may also be prepared to quote from a favourite poem or extract in his welcome to the congregation or in the sermon.

Music

MUSIC IS A very important part of the wedding cere-mony, except in Quaker celebrations. It sets the mood and is chosen for its joyful qualities, or to add a note of majesty as the bride and her groom arrive and depart from church.

For a traditional Christian wedding, you will probably be accompanied by the church organ, so the music you choose must suit this instrument and the skills of the organist. Speak to the organist to find out what he or she can play and whether they have any suggestions. If you want music as part of a civil marriage, remember that it cannot have any religious associations. You may prefer to use popular, recorded music anyway – perhaps the first song you ever danced to together or a song that epitomis-es your feelings for one another. Discuss the use of music with the registrar before the wedding day.

It is traditional in most Christian ceremonies to have entry music for the bride and exit music for the bride and groom, two or three hymns, and an instrumental or choral piece while the register is being signed – often out of sight in the sacristy. When choosing hymns, read the words carefully – although it is popular, you may not be keen on "dark satanic mills" even if you do like the tune of *Jerusalem*. Also be careful that the hymns are reasonably well known because, unless you have a choir, you will be

Popular entry and exit music

Entry music for the bride

Arrival of the Queen of Sheba	Handel
Music for the Royal Fireworks	Handel
Bridal March	Parry
Grand March from Aida	Verdi
Bridal March from Lohengrin	Wagner
("Here Comes the Bride")	

Exit music for the couple

Trumpet Voluntary	Boyce
Trumpet Voluntary	Clarke
Trumpet tune and air	Purcell
Toccata in C	Pachabel
Wedding March from	
A Midsummer Night's Dream	Mendelssohn
Toccata from Symphony No.5	
in F Major	Widor

disappointed if nobody sings. Pitch is also something you should discuss with the organist or any accompanists that you use. For the music during the signing of the register, you may like to choose something very personal to you as a couple, which may mean modern or popular music sung or played by friends if the minister or priest is agreeable. Remember that if you hire a professional choir, you will have to pay them, usually per head; a soloist adds to the expense, as does recorded music.

Flowers

FLOWERS ARE A FEATURE at most weddings, although, of course, the number, colour and style is a matter of personal preference and budget. Traditionally, they signify spring and new birth and are a symbol of fertility. In the past, strong smelling herbs were strewn before the bride as they were thought to ward off ill health, bad luck and evil spirits.

Flowers can be very expensive, depending on the kind of flowers you choose and the number and type of arrangements that you have. The bride and any bridesmaids usually carry a bouquet each and may wear flowers in their hair; the groom, best man and other important male guests wear buttonholes; and the mothers of the bride and groom wear corsages. Other floral decorations include arrangements at the church or registry office, which might include pedestal arrangements, pew ends and doorway bowers. Larger arrangements can usually be taken on and used to decorate the reception.

In some registry offices, there may be a floral arrangement already in place, and for church weddings, if there is another wedding before or after your own, it is often worth getting in touch with the other bride to see if she wants to share the cost of the flowers. You may also choose to have table arrangements at the reception – make sure they don't get in the way of conversation.

Choosing your flowers requires a lot of thought. To choose the size, shape and colour of your bouquet, you should consider your favourite shades, your figure and colouring (and those of your bridesmaids if their bouquets reflect yours), the style and fabric of your dress and the colours of those of your bridesmaids, as well as the overall effect that you would like to achieve. The architecture of the church or reception venue and the amount of indoor light may also have an impact on your choice.

The meaning of flowers

Consider choosing flowers for their symbolism.

bluebell	everlasting love
camellia	loveliness
daisy	innocence
hyacinth	playfulness
ivy	fidelity
jonquil	returned affection
lily of the valley	happiness
mimosa	secret love
orchid	beauty
ornamental cabbage	profit
carnation	a woman in love
red tulip	love
rose	romance
stephanotis	travel
tuberrose	voluptuousness
violet	faithfulness

3

What kind of reception?

❧

A WEDDING RECEPTION is not simply a good excuse for a party; it has a symbolic purpose – in medieval times it was a chance for the groom to show he could look after his wife by giving gifts of food to his future in-laws.

You need to think about your reception very soon after you get engaged. Hotels and other venues tend to be fully booked for months, so you must book six to nine months in advance if you want a particular venue. Don't be left with only disappointing or expensive choices.

Crucial considerations

- Budget is the venue affordable?
- Size of venue – can the space accommodate all your guests?
- Reception drinks – can you have them outdoors if the weather is sunny and warm?
- Photos – is there somewhere suitable for taking photographs?
- Food – can the venue supply the meal you want, whether a buffet or a three-course meal?
- Decor – what colours and types of crockery, tablecloths and lighting will you choose?

- Entertainment or music – does the venue supply?
- What time does the venue stay open until?
- Children – is there room or provision for?
- Package deal – does the quote include cake, toastmaster, flowers and a room to change in?

Organising your own reception

Rather than booking a venue, you may choose to have your reception at home, either in the house or in a marquee. Home receptions are popular as they tend to be more personal, save on the cost of a venue and mark-ups on drinks, and allow flexibility in terms of food, decor and timing. They do involve more planning and work, however. If you wish to use a marquee, go by recommendation if possible, and always obtain several quotes from local companies. Check what's included in the price, and how long you will have the marquee.

Choosing a marquee

Consider the following:
- *Size and colour of marquee*
- *Tables and chairs – do they provide?*
- *Dance floor*
- *Lighting*
- *Flowers and decoration*
- *Heating – even in summer, marquees get cold later in the evening*
- *Toilet facilities*

Catering considerations

WHATEVER THE VENUE you choose, you'll need to think carefully about what kind of food and drink you want to provide, whether it's a four-course sit-down dinner or simply canapés and drinks. Hotels and many other venues will insist on using their own caterers, and most will offer a range of set meals priced per head. Make sure you have a meal at your chosen venue before you make your final decision. In fact, it's a good idea to eat there more than once to check that the food and wine and service are of an acceptable and consistent standard.

Be sure to check the cost of the drinks, as this is often the most expensive part; you may be able to supply your own, although the hotel will charge corkage. You may prefer to provide some of the drinks at the reception but also have a paying bar; this is a good budgeting measure. Remember to ask about meals for children and arrange for them to eat earlier if necessary.

Choosing a caterer

If you have decided to hold the reception at home, contact several caterers, ideally on personal recommendations, and consider a selection of ideas and prices. Give each caterer an idea of the number of guests and what kind of meal you have in mind – hot or cold food, sit-down meal or finger buffet, one or three courses.

Caterer checklist

Make sure you discuss each of the following points with each potential caterer:
- *Different menus and variations*
- *Price range per head*
- *Waitressing*
- *Drinks – who supplies and serves*
- *Cutlery and plates, glassware etc*
- *Tablecloths*
- *Timing*
- *A buffet for after-dinner guests*

Self-catering

You might want to take charge of the catering yourself, particularly if you've had experience in doing large parties. While this might seem a cost-effective and flexible option, do bear in mind that the run-up to the wedding is likely to be hectic, and you'll need to prepare well in advance. Self-catering can be very time-consuming and stressful.

Don't take on more than you can handle and make sure that you will have plenty of help both on the day and beforehand during the preparations.

You'll need to think about:

- *Help and support.* If it's an informal and personal occasion, and the cost is an issue, you could ask friends and family to get involved and each bring a designated dish instead of a present.
- *Storage* – where will you keep everything fresh until the day? Can you borrow space in a neighbour's freezer for a few weeks?
- *Cutlery, plates and glassware* – will you need to borrow or hire this? You'll also need tablecloths and napkins. Some companies hire out china, cutlery, glassware etc as well as other catering equipment, such as fridges.
- *Seats and tables* (if you're doing a sit-down meal). If it's a buffet you'll need trestle tables to display the food. You may also need a cake stand.
- *Waitresses* to help serve, clear away and wash up.
- Special meals – do you need to organise meals for children or vegetarians?

Above all, don't be too ambitious. Aim to keep things simple: carefully prepared and well-presented food can be just as delicious – and probably less stressful – to prepare than an unfamiliar *cordon bleu* menu.

Deciding on the drinks

The venue you choose, the type of meal you decide upon, the number of guests you invite and your overall budget will together determine the type and quantity of the drinks you serve.

Champagne is popular at weddings, but the cost of supplying your guests with an endless stream of bubbly can be prohibitive. You'll need to allow two to three glasses per guest when everyone is arriving at the reception. One alternative is to serve wine throughout the reception, reserving the champagne for the speeches and toasts only. If you opt for this, allow one to two glasses per guest.

There are some very reasonably priced champagnes available – keep an eye out for special offers at supermarkets and wine merchants. Also, you can serve sparkling wines and cavas instead of champagne.

If you're having a summer wedding, you could consider something a bit different, such as Pimms with fruit, which makes a pretty alternative and is refreshing on a hot day. For a winter wedding, mulled wine makes a warming greeting drink. Make sure there are soft drinks available at all times for people not drinking alcohol and for children. It's worth putting jugs of water on the tables during the meal.

Planning a buffet

A BUFFET IS A POPULAR choice at weddings, offering great freedom of choice and less formality than a sit-down meal. People often assume it's the less expensive option. However, this is not necessarily the case – so look at budgets for both kinds of catering.

For best results be inventive and combine seasonal ingredients cleverly. A buffet doesn't need to mean french bread and dull salads. There are masses of dishes you might like to consider, from cooked ham, whole salmon or side of beef to the more informal fish and chips. For a summer barbecue, a pig roast can be wonderful with salads and sauces; while a winter wedding might suggest curry, rice and popadoms. Alternatively you might prefer a wedding breakfast of bacon and eggs or a wedding afternoon tea of delicate sandwiches, scones and cakes.

A buffet is not constrained by a formal menu and offers a wide range of food. This is an advantage if you do your own catering. An Italian theme might include a table of cold starters, followed by a lasagna, while a traditional Scandinavian smorgasbord could allow you to mix and match flavours with a varied array of savoury foods, including fish, meat and cold vegetable dishes.

Things to consider:

• *Budget*

• *Season*
A summer wedding suggests lighter dishes while a more hearty, warming meal would probably be welcome in winter. Think about what is in season, from strawberries and asparagus through to winter fruits.

• *Quantity*
Make sure you don't scrimp – there's nothing worse than running out.

• *Serving*
Even for a buffet, it's quicker and more efficient to have people serving out the food. Ushers can tell guests at each table when to go up for food. It's a good idea to have two serving areas if possible to avoid guests waiting for a long time or a dreadful crush.

• *Appearance*
Fresh herbs, watercress, edible flowers, such as borage and young nasturtiums, make dishes look appealing. Kiwi fruits and coloured berries are great for decoration, while fresh fruit salad with cream or ice cream always makes a refreshing, pretty dessert.

Planning a sit-down meal

W HETHER YOU'RE at a hotel, in a marquee or at home, you may prefer to have a sit-down meal with serving staff at each table. Depending on the timing of your wedding, you will choose a wedding breakfast or brunch, a light lunch or a three- or four-course supper. A sit-down meal doesn't necessarily have to be highly formal; actress Kate Winslet famously chose bangers and mash for her wedding meal, but most of us would prefer something a little more festive.

A traditional meal

If you decide upon a traditional three-course meal, it's a good idea to choose a starter that can stand for a while without spoiling, as it often takes longer than you think to get everyone seated. If you're having a fairly light starter, you might like to follow it with a sorbet to cleanse the palate before the main course. In addition, you could set on the table a variety of unusual breads, such as foccaccia or ciabatta, with saucers of olive oil and bowls of olives.

Choose a main dish you know most people will like – there's no point being adventurous with scallops or quail if no one's going to eat it. Chicken, fish, lamb, salmon and beef all tend to be popular. Equally, it's best to avoid rich or very spicy sauces.

If your budget doesn't run to fancy desserts, your wedding cake should be quite sufficient. Accompany it with some fresh fruit salad or cream. *Petits fours* with coffee make a nice end to the meal.

The wedding cake

There are a few traditions surrounding the wedding cake. Cutting the cake together is a symbolic act, supposed to prevent a childless marriage; keeping a piece of cake is said to guarantee your husband's fidelity. Many couples keep the top tier for the christening of their first child – it's possible to keep a fruit wedding cake for several years if you freeze it.

If you prefer, you can steer away from the traditional rich fruit cake and choose instead chocolate and cream: one recent bride chose a mountain of white chocolate profiteroles. Or you might like your cake to be composed of several different flavoured layers to suit all tastes – lemon, banana, vanilla, chocolate, coffee.

Be as inventive as you like. Have sugar models made of yourself and the groom or of your bouquet to place on the top. Use coloured ribbons, real flowers and foliage for decoration. The cake can be as many tiers as you like and any shape you like; and it can be presented on a stand, stacked or set on pillars.

Decorating the reception venue

The decorations for the reception should be in keeping with the style and formality of the whole wedding. A grand hotel or a stately home will call for elegant and formal flower arrangements, perhaps reflecting the period in which the hotel or stately home was built. A home reception, perhaps held in a marquee, will call for less formal arrangements.

If you have chosen a special theme for your wedding, reflecting the season, a particular interest or hobby or your favourite historical period, then you will want to continue this theme at the reception venue. A winter wonderland wedding, for example, will suggest plenty of red, green and gold touches in the decorations; a Renaissance theme – which led you to choose a castle for your reception venue – will demand flower arrangements in period style, and perhaps call for herbs to be strewn over the stone floor and crushed underfoot.

Positioning the flowers

You will need to place flowers at the entrance to the reception, by the receiving line, around the edges of the room and on the tables. Tall or large table centrepieces make it difficult for guests to talk to one another across the tables and may obscure guests' view of the top table. So, try to keep these arrangements low – small rustic baskets perhaps – or use single flower vases to create a restrained but elegant look. Pedestal arrangements generally look good set against large, blank wall spaces. And garlands, swags and arches are ideal wrapped around the posts of a marquee or draped along the edge of a long top table.

Be creative!

If you're at home or in a marquee think of some unusual ways of creating atmosphere, such as using fairy lights or floating candles. Always steer clear of bright overhead lights which are unflattering and unromantic. Incorporate some of the garden inside the marquee in the form of flowers or pot plants to create a natural transition.

Be as creative as possible with the decorations while keeping to your colour theme. Tie flowers or balloons to the backs of chairs and think of inventive ways to present the placecards – hand write them in coloured inks, decorate them with flowers, clip them onto each plate with a peg. Use coloured twine, grass or ribbon for napkin rings.

Write out menus in coloured ink and roll into a scroll tied with ribbon or coloured twine. Place glass bowls of Smarties or coloured sugared almond favours on the tables. Alternatively, scatter over the tables sequins, rose petals, heart-shaped coloured papers, gold and silver glitter, tiny shells for a seaside theme or herbs – such as lavender and rosemary – for a country theme.

Entertainment

W EDDING ENTERTAINMENT can range from a string quartet during drinks to a rock and roll band after the meal. Other entertainments include fireworks, a magician or a even a roulette table. Check the bridal magazines' classified section for agencies.

Music is important at a wedding. One bride asked each guest to write their three favourite songs on their reply card. Do you want music during the early part of the reception, when guests are arriving and having a drink? Some people find a string quartet, a jazz trio or even a harpist can add to the atmosphere. If you have a talented musician in the family, perhaps they'll play for a while.

If you intend to hire a disco, go and see a few DJs in action before booking one. Compare prices and check what time they are prepared to play until. If you want to be absolutely sure that the music they play is what you want, give them a list. Try to make sure there's something for everyone. If you're hiring a band, go and listen to them beforehand. Think about timing and how long they will play for. Consider the noise level that is appropriate to the venue – will the sound stop all coversation? Will there be room for all the equipment and speakers?

Whichever you choose, it's traditional for the bride and groom to take the first dance, so you'll need to choose a song that you both like and that is possible to dance to. If the thought of dancing in front of your guests fills you with dread, book a few dance lessons beforehand.

A dramatic send-off for the bride and groom can be memorable. If you have plenty of outdoor space, a few fireworks will provide a magical finale, or you could give a sparkler to each guest. You might prefer to have bag-pipes playing, or a mass of balloons and streamers let off.

Hen night

• *Decide which friends you want to attend your hen night and let them know well in advance. Some pubs and hotels do not welcome large groups, so be sure to check your venue beforehand.*

• *Don't have it the night before the wedding. Leave at least two weeks to recover!*

• *Consult every member of the group to agree on a budget, and stick to it, so that everyone can relax and enjoy themselves.*

• *Talk through ideas with your chief bridesmaid. Do you want an evening or a weekend party? Will you spend it in the town or the country? Options range from adventurous pursuits such as dancing or sailing to a picnic in the park or a day at a health farm.*

• *Book taxis well in advance to avoid getting stranded on the night.*

• *Traditionally, the best man organises a stag night for the groom.*

4

Getting down to details

❧❦❧

IN ADDITION TO DECIDING when and where you want to get married and what kind of reception you will have, there are a host of decisions and arrangements to be made in the run up to the wedding. You will also need to mastermind and coordinate events on the big day.

The guest list must be decided upon and the invitations printed and sent out. You need to compile a wedding list of presents you would like to get so that you don't receive 15 toasters and 23 sets of towels and that the individual pieces of dinner service match one another. The photographer and transport have to be organised. And, of course, you must select your dress and the groom's outfit and determine the attire of the rest of the wedding party. Gifts must be bought for your attendants, and you must choose and book your hairdresser and the person who will do your make-up.

Traditionally, the bride and groom appoint a team of helpers, known as attendants, to assist them with many of the arrangements and to ensure the actual day goes according to plan. Of course, both the bride and groom's parents will want to play a part in making the day run smoothly, although it's generally best if they can relax and enjoy it as much as possible. The bride's mother usually co-ordinates the wedding, particularly if the reception is taking place at the bride's home. If they haven't already done so, arrange for both sets of parents to meet before the big day.

The groom's attendants

Soon after getting engaged, the groom should choose the best man – usually his closest friend or a brother. The best man's role is an important one, not just in terms of organisation and speech-making but also in supplying moral support at all times. The groom needs to choose someone who will be responsible, confident and helpful, able to deal with friends and relatives of all ages. His main tasks will be arranging the stag night or weekend, arranging transport to and from church, looking after the rings and honeymoon documentation and generally ensuring that events run smoothly, so you don't have to worry.

His most nerve-wracking role is making a speech at the reception. The best man's speech is notoriously difficult to get right. For best results he should keep the speech brief and genuine, avoid cheap laughs at the groom's expense and go easy on the champagne until afterwards. In his speech he should thank the groom for his toast to the bridesmaids, talk about the groom and toast the couple.

For a formal church wedding, the groom should also choose at least three ushers. Again, they must be reliable and confident and either brothers of the bride or groom or close friends. The ushers' role is to support the best man, helping hand out service sheets and seat people in church, and then helping to arrange transport from the church to the reception. They might also assist the photographer to organise friends and family for pictures.

The bride's attendants

As soon as possible after getting engaged, you should choose your bridesmaids, who can be adults, children or a mix of both. The chief bridesmaid, normally a close friend or a sister, will be responsible for helping you in any way that is useful in your preparations for the wedding, such as choosing your dress and the bridesmaids' outfits and attending the fittings, helping you to keep a note of acceptances and gifts as they arrive. She will also attend to you throughout the day, calming your nerves, helping you to dress and holding your bouquet during the ceremony. She will look after any young bridesmaids on the day and organise the hen night. Consequently it is essential that she has a calm and efficient personality! The number of bridesmaids you have is entirely up to you, although bear in mind that you may be paying for their outfits.

If you decide to have little sisters, cousins or god-children as attendants, make sure their mothers are sitting nearby during the ceremony in case of a bad attack of nerves. You might like to have one young bridesmaid act as a flower girl, dropping rose petals as you walk down the aisle; others could hand out boxes of confetti to the guests. Remember to buy your bridesmaids gifts, such as silver bracelets or chains, to thank them for their assistance and participation.

Discuss outfits with your bridesmaids well in advance. Talk through your preferred colours and styles to make sure they will be relaxed about what they will be wearing. The cost of their attire may be borne by the bride, but sometimes bridesmaids buy their own outfits. They will need new shoes and a posy of flowers. You might want them to have special make-up and visit the hairdresser.

Who does what at the wedding

Bridegroom

- *Makes speech after the bride's father, thanking the bride's parents for the wedding and the guests for their attendance*
- *Proposes toast to the bridesmaid(s)*
- *Thanks the best man*

Ushers

- *Greet guests as they arrive at the church*
- *Hand out service sheets to them*
- *Guide them to their seats*
- *Help best man organise transport for guests to the reception*
- *Chief usher takes care of the bride's mother and groom's parents and escorts them to their seats*

Best man

- Ensures that buttonholes and service sheets are at the church
- Makes sure the groom's going-away clothes are at the hotel or reception venue
- Gets groom to the church on time
- Pays the church fees on groom's behalf
- Brings rings to the church; hands them to the groom during ceremony
- Arranges lifts from church to reception and is last to leave for the reception
- Helps marshal friends and family for photographs
- Announces speeches and cutting of the cake
- Makes speech; reads out cards, telegrams and messages
- If groom is changing, ensures that his formal dress is looked after and returned
- Arranges transport for bride and groom from the reception

Bride's father

- Drives to church with the bride
- Walks down the aisle with the bride and gives her away
- Makes first speech at reception, welcoming guests and proposing a toast to bride and groom

Chief bridesmaid

- *Helps bride to dress*
- *Takes charge of younger bridesmaids, ensuring that they are dressed correctly and that each has the right bouquet*
- *Ensures bride's veil and train are in place for the walk down the aisle*
- *Takes bride's bouquet during the ceremony, returning it after the signing of the register*
- *Helps bride change into going-away outfit and looks after her wedding dress*

The Mothers

- *Help bride to dress*
- *Help with smaller bridesmaids*
- *Attend the signing of the register*
- *Aid bridesmaid with any presents brought to wedding*
- *Stay until last guests depart*

Invitations

S OON AFTER YOU have determined the budget you should compile a guest list, consulting both your own and the groom's parents. Your invitations should reflect the overall style and tone of your wedding, whether it's traditional or innovative, formal or informal. If you have chosen to build your wedding around a particular historical period or interest, then the invitations should be in keeping.

• Ask printers and design companies for samples and compare quotes.

• Think about reply cards, order of service sheets, place cards, menus, evening invitations and thank-you cards. Can you get a discount if you order in bulk?

• Order invitations and envelopes around four months beforehand. Remember you only need one invite per couple. Order extra in case of mistakes.

• Send out invitations three months before the wedding date; it is courteous to send an invitation to the groom's parents.

• For guests who live far away, enclose a list of local hotels and bed and breakfasts with the invitation, as well as a map showing the church and reception venue, and provide local taxi numbers.

• Alternatively, let your guests know if your friends and relations can accommodate them. Let everyone involved know how to get in touch with each other.

The traditional invitation wording for both a church service and a civil wedding is as follows.

> *Mr and Mrs Michael Rigby*
> *request the pleasure of your company at the*
> *marriage of their daughter*
> *Sarah Jane*
> *to Mr James Harper*
>
> *at*
> *St Mary's Church, Tickhill*
> *on Saturday 18 July, 1999*
> *at 2 p.m.*
>
> *and afterwards at*
> *The White Lodge, Tickhill*
>
> *RSVP*
> *Address to respond to*

If the bride's mother has remarried: Mr Michael Rigby and Mrs Anne Thomas request the pleasure…

The bride's parents are divorced but still sharing surname: Mr Michael Rigby and Mrs Anne Rigby…

The bride's (widowed) mother is host: Mrs Michael Rigby

The bride's mother is widowed/divorced and remarried: Mr and Mrs Chris Thomas request … at the marriage of her daughter…

The bride's father is remarried: Mr and Mrs Michael Rigby request … at the marriage of his daughter…

Wedding gifts

THE CUSTOM OF GIVING wedding presents started as a way of helping young couples set up home together, so presents were useful household items. The tradition continues today – even for those couples who may already have a home – and gifts range from potato peelers to bed linen, mirrors to television sets.

Most guests will phone you or your mother to find out what presents would be appreciated. For this reason, it is vital for you and your fiancé to prepare your list before the wedding invitations are sent out. When compiling your list, make sure that the price range is wide and the choice of items varied so that last-minute shoppers are not left with one choice – the porcelain dinner service.

Most large department stores run bridal registries. They supply you with a form in which to write the items you want, allowing you to wander through the shop as you make your decisions. The store then keeps the list and guests phone or visit the store to select an item from it to be sent to you. To ensure there is no duplication, the store ticks off purchases as they are made. They then deliver the gifts, carefully marked with the purchaser's name, to the address you supply them with – try to ensure that there will generally be someone to accept the parcels at the address you provide. Traditionally, gifts are sent to the bride or the bride's mother.

Sample wedding list

KITCHEN
corkscrew
wooden spoons
spatula
toaster
microwave oven
measuring spoons
mugs
fridge
freezer
saucepans
steak knives
frying pan
blender
apron
chopping board
bread basket
kettle
washing machine
storage jars
coffee maker

DINING ROOM
dinner service
silver service
vegetable dishes
table linen
place mats
jam pot
fruit bowl

wine glasses
carafe
ice bucket
wine cooler
cream jug
glassware
decanters

SITTING ROOM
standard lamp
candlesticks
scatter cushions
rug
CD player
television
magazine rack
fireplace tools
sofa

BEDROOM
bed
bed linen
blanket box
duvet
duvet cover
radio alarm
bedside lamp
electric blanket
sheets
pillow cases

bedspread
pillows
mirror

BATHROOM
towels
mirror
waste bin
bath rack
scales
cabinet

GARDEN
barbecue set
electric drill
wheelbarrow
washing line
furniture
tools
lawn mower

OTHERS
picture frames
clock
doormat
vases
luggage
lamps
photo albums

For those couples who already have a well-equipped home

candlesticks
prints
rugs
vases
glassware
specialist kitchen items such as a pasta maker or espresso machine
antique china plate or cups and saucers
gift vouchers

Displaying the gifts

It is an old custom to display the wedding gifts, usually in your parents' home. Prepare one room where guests can easily walk about and look at the presents. The display should be tactfully arranged, so that gifts are not made to look obviously inexpensive, or those that are similar are not put too close together. It is quite in order to show only one place setting from a dinner service, or one set of towels from a double set. Cards with the names of the donors should be placed next to each item.

Be very careful about displaying the gifts in a public place, such as the reception venue, as this may cost you a large sum in guards and insurance. Feel free to drop this custom if you think the gift display reveals a wide price range that might embarrass some of your guests.

Although it is the custom for gifts to be sent before the wedding, some guests are bound to arrive at the reception with their presents. Ask your chief bridesmaid or the best man to take care of these. Ensure that there is a table where they can be placed. If the party is being held at a hotel or similar public venue, you will also need to make sure that the gifts are kept in a safe, secure place and that the best man takes them to your home or your mother's home after the reception.

Thanking guests for their gifts

There are two ways of thanking your friends for their presents. One is to write a thank you note immediately after each gift is delivered; the other is to sit down after your wedding with a list of guests and the presents they sent and send your notes in bulk. This method can become a huge chore, and there is always a risk of forgetting who sent what or losing the card originally attached to the present so that you don't know whom to thank.

Printed "thank you" cards are available but it is preferable to send a personal, handwritten note – especially as a wedding is an occasion where most people go to considerable effort and expense to give you something you really need. Whichever system you follow, use a copy of your guest list with the addresses to record what each guest sent you. Then, as you send off your thank-you notes, you can tick that name off on the list. It is your mother's enviable task to pack and store your gifts until you return from your honeymoon!

Gifts for your team and guests

TRADITIONALLY THE bride and groom show their appreciation for the contributions of their attendants and their parents in making the wedding a success by giving presents to each member of the team. Strictly speaking the groom pays for the gifts, although today many couples share the expense.

Traditional gifts

The chief bridesmaid is often given jewellery she can wear at the wedding, such as a pretty necklace or earrings to suit her outfit. Of course, jewellery isn't the only choice. Watches, compacts, atomizers and jewellery cases are perfect and can easily be personalised with an engraving as a permanent reminder of the day. For younger bridemaids there is a wide choice of heart-shaped lockets, flower pendants, crosses and gold or silver bracelets.

The best man is usually presented with a special gift as his role is key to the smooth running of the day. Consider giving him a silver or leather hip flask, pewter mug, desk clock, cufflinks or a leather stud box. The ushers and pageboys might appreciate desk clocks, watches, clock radios, cufflinks or key rings.

The groom will probably want to give your mother his own gift to commemorate her daughter's wedding day. Jewellery is once again the obvious choice as it can be treasured for years and will be a constant reminder of the happy union. He may select a wonderful pearl necklace, or an elegant brooch. Or he may choose a ring or a bracelet with your names or initials, and the wedding date engraved on the inner curve.

Traditionally all the gifts for the wedding party are presented before the wedding so that the jewellery can be worn with the bridal outfits. You and your fiancé may hold an informal supper party or a formal dinner after the wedding rehearsal, which would be an appropriate time to make the presentations. On the other hand, you may prefer to use the reception as the occasion to show your gratitude to the wedding team and present them with their gifts then.

Wedding favours

Some couples follow the Italian wedding custom of giving each of the guests a "wedding favour". This is a little printed box or ribboned, tulle bag filled with sugared almonds which is placed at each guest's seat at the reception tables. You may prefer to give miniature drams of whisky with a personalised label printed with your names and the wedding date. Novelty presents, such as ceramic or paper teddies, top hats and bonnets are also available from specialised wedding services. But check your budget before you take on this extra expense.

Organising the photography

CHOOSING THE RIGHT photographer to take the pictures for your wedding is one of the most important decisions you will have to make. After all, many brides have remarked that their wedding day – so much anticipated and planned for – goes by in a whirl. But good photographs will be there to look at and enjoy forever.

Employing a professional

If you plan to use a professional photographer you will need to choose and book one as early as possible. Good wedding photographers get booked up far in advance.

Before choosing your photographer ask for brochures or portfolios from a wide range of professional wedding photographers. Contact a professional body such as the Master Photographers Association for details of their members in your area. Recommendations from friends, of course, are often the most valuable.

Make sure that you have an in-depth discussion with the photographer that you eventually choose. Talk to him about the sort of pictures you require, and the sort of poses you like and don't like. A good photographer will take the time to gain your confidence, so that you will be relaxed in the pictures he eventually takes. Photographers often do not attend the reception. If you want yours to be there, make sure you arrange it in advance.

Discuss what will happen if he should be ill on the day. Does he have a back-up photographer available? And what if the photographs go wrong in any way? Make sure the photographer has adequate insurance.

You will also need to find out what wedding packages are available. For a set fee, some photographers will attend the wedding and include a fixed number of prints. Others quote a fee to attend the wedding and charge for the photographs on top. You should also find out whether you or the photographer keeps the wedding proofs and how long it will be before the photographs are developed.

Agree the charges in writing and pay a deposit, making sure you work out when the final charges should be paid.

Taking your own photographs

Sometimes, particularly if your budget is tight, well-meaning friends will offer to take the wedding pictures. On the whole, this is not advisable unless you have no other option, or they are professional photographers. Your friends are likely to take pictures anyway, but they will want to concentrate on being wedding guests, rather than trying to find the best angle for a picture. Relying on friends could also – at worst – mean you have no good pictures of your special day.

When choosing a photographer, you need to work out what style of photographs you want. Do you want traditional, posed photographs? What about a "reportage" style of pictures, where the photographer follows guests around and takes more candid shots? Do you want colour pictures, or the more unusual and evocative photographs you will get with black and white?

If you want a really wide range of "natural" shots, place a disposable camera on each table at the reception so that guests can take photographs themselves. This also adds an extra element of fun to the day, and the photos will show you aspects of your wedding that you missed.

Checklist of poses

Talk with your professional photographer about the type of poses you would like to have taken. They may include:

Before the ceremony: Bride alone; with mother; with father; with both parents; bride with her attendants; bride adjusting veil; bride getting into the wedding car.
Groom alone; with the best man and ushers; with his parents.
Guests arriving; bridesmaids; bride's mother; bride arriving with her father.

During the ceremony (if permitted): Bride and her father walking down the aisle; signing the register.

After the ceremony: Couple at the church door; bride

alone; groom alone; bride and groom; bride, groom, best man and chief bridesmaids; bride, groom and attendants; bride, groom and registrar/minister; bride, groom and parents; the full wedding party; bride and groom getting into the car; wedding party throwing confetti.

And, of course, shots of the groom with his family and of you with your relatives.

The reception: Couple arriving; receiving guests; with parents; the speeches; cutting the cake; bride and groom's first dance; bride throwing the bouquet; "going away".

Videotaping the event

Many couples also want a video recording of their wedding. Hire a company specialising in wedding videos. An experienced amateur with a good quality camera may also be satisfactory.

Ministers sometimes – but not always – allow cere-monies to be videotaped. If you want your marriage videoed, then make sure you find out if this is allowed. If it is, you should visit the church beforehand with the videographer in order to check the lighting.

Whether you have a professional or amateur video, remember that it will also need to be well-edited, as you will not want to watch hours and hours of people eating and chatting. Titling or dubbed-in music are included in a professional video, and it is not likely that you will find an amateur who can offer this service.

Considering the transport

M ANY WEDDING CAR specialists are booked a year in advance, particularly those that supply unusual limousines in a wide choice of colours. So you have to make some important decisions long before the big day if you want a proper quote that covers all your needs.

You want to arrive at your wedding in style – a quaint vintage car or a classic automobile are popular choices, and some couples choose a coach and horses. Make sure the vehicle you choose is large enough to sit in without crumpling your dress. You will need one car to take you and your father from your home to the wedding service, and another for your mother and the bridesmaids. Will they require two cars?

You will require several cars to take the wedding party from the service to the reception. In addition to you and the groom, both sets of parents and the bridesmaids, you may need to arrange transport for elderly relatives. If your wedding is to take place in a remote, romantic spot will your guests need a minibus to take them there?

Decide all these factors before you start phoning car hire companies, and ask each one about special deals for hiring numerous cars for long periods of time. Ask if the chauffeur will be wearing a uniform and how much extra that will cost? Will the hire company decorate the car with ribbons in the front and flowers at the rear? Consider whether you desire these decorations and ask what the cost will be of having them.

When you have decided which hire company to use, send them a clear map of the route you want the cars to follow. You will probably be very nervous on the day and not in the mood for giving instructions to the chauffeur.

A wedding procession is difficult to organise in town, but a bride and groom in the country can lead their guests down a country lane from the church to the reception.

No matter what form of transport you choose, ask your best man to ensure that a clutch of umbrellas is on hand to protect you and your attendants against rainy weather.

Leaving the reception

When it's time to leave the party and be on your way, you can, of course, simply leave by car. For the bride and groom who are looking to make a splashier exit, however, there are plenty of creative alternatives to consider. Couples over the years have chosen to leave by hot air balloon, motorcycle, tractor, horse and carriage, rowboat, motor boat, gondola, train, bus and by other unusual modes of transport.

Choosing your wedding outfit

THIS IS YOUR WEDDING and you can wear whatever fits your dream, your shape and your colouring. You intend to look your radiant best. Your dress should set the tone of your wedding. An ornate gown with a long train will not suit the mood, or the clothes, of your guests at a civil marriage in the municipal offices followed by a reception at a pub.

Start looking for your dress months before the day. Take your mother and your chief bridesmaid to visit bridal shops and try on dresses in all sorts of styles and materials. You will soon find the styles that suit you, and discover whether white, cream or ivory flatters your skin tone. You will see how silk, satin or crepe-de-chine affects the cut of a dress.

Not all brides choose to walk down the aisle wearing white. Pastels are becoming increasingly popular. You can find dresses highlighted with peaches, golds, yellows, lavenders, light pinks and baby blues. The colour might be used sparingly in the tulle, the beading or the fabric flowers, or the dress itself can be made of a coloured or patterned fabric. You may even find deep crimson velvet makes you look wonderful.

Fine fabrics

Batiste	*Soft, fine cotton*
Brocade	*Raised design in the same colour as background*
Chintz	*Glazed cotton usually with a floral design*
Crepe	*Slightly crinkled silk or cotton with a strong draping quality*
Organza	*Transparent, slightly stiff and shiny*
Raw silk	*Silk with a noticeable weave*
Satin	*Heavy, smooth and glossy*
Tulle	*Fine netting*

Once you have discovered the gown that matches your fantasies, you have to make the dream fit the budget. Will you have a made-to-measure designer dress or buy off the peg? Will you hire a frock, or go to a dressmaker? If you are having something specially made, book the designer or dressmaker at least four months in advance.

Ensure that the bridesmaids' dresses flatter each of them while also complementing your gown. Their dress colours and accessories should reflect the floral and table decorations. Let pageboys wear something they can run and jump in.

Accessories

You are going to spend a lot of time standing, walking and dancing at your wedding. So make sure your wedding shoes are comfortable as well as gorgeous, and wear them at home before the day to break them in. The shape of your gown will determine the length of your veil and the height of your hat, tiara or floral headgear. So, if possible, choose these while you are fitting the dress. Most bridal boutiques stock these accessories.

Veils. Made of fine, transparent cloth, such as tulle, these can be attached to a band or tiara. If your dress has no train, your veil should be short, dropping to the shoulders, waist or fingertips. A long veil should extend about 40 cm beyond a train.

Hats. These can be worn with the wisp of a veil, or simply be decorative, balancing the size and line of the wedding outfit. A big brimmed hat will obscure your face in the photographs, and could cause a certain awkwardness when the groom wants to kiss you.

Flowers. In preference to the traditional all-white bouquet, you might choose to carry an informal country-style bouquet, bunches of berries, flowering branches, sprays of wheat, a simple nosegay of rosemary or an armful of long-stemmed roses. For a dramatic look a single flower such as a giant lily or orchid is effective. A garland of flowers can be worn around the neck.

Flowers can also adorn shoes or be tucked into a bun on your head. Pinned among curls, tracing a chignon or

Fashion terms

A-line skirt	*Narrow and close fitting at waist, flaring out towards hem*
Ballerina skirt	*Ankle-length, full, gathered skirt*
Bell sleeves	*Long sleeves, narrow at the shoulder flaring out at wrist*
Bodice	*Top half of dress*
Bolero	*Waist-length jacket, no collar and no fastenings*
Bustle	*Gathered, puffed construction on back waistline*
Dropped waist	*Bodice extended below natural waistline*
Juliet cap	*Fitted cap worn on the back of the head*

woven into a band, flowers are a charming accessory. Real or artificial flowers scattered in your hair will demand the skill of your hairdresser, so add time to your preparations on the day.

Other Options. There are pretty, sparkling hair grips and combs on the market, ornamented with butterfly, shell, flower, star and leaf motifs. If you wish to decorate your hair with these, remember that most are not sturdy enough to carry a veil.

Hair and make-up matters

THREE MONTHS BEFORE the wedding, visit your hair-dresser. Make sure you are confident about her skills and that she can style your hair to complement your dress and accessories. Not many hairdressers have experience in piling-up and curling hair in elaborate fashion, but such a look may ideally suit your wedding outfit.

Talk to her about the headdress you have chosen, or better still, take the tiara, veil or hat with you. Tell her how you want your hair to look, and listen to her when she tempers your fantasy with sensible advice. She will have to think carefully about how to style short hair that will be decorated with a tiara or flowers.

Book your hairdresser for the day well in advance. Can she come round to your home? Is she far from where you live? Will she do the chief bridesmaid's hair as well?

Have a few practice runs to test different hair and make-up styles. Ask your bridesmaid to take photographs of each experiment and check what styles enhance your face and your headdress. Wear something in the colour of your gown, or wrap a white towel about your shoulders. Bear in mind that you want your make-up to look good

for hours in both natural and artificial light. You will probably not have time to freshen up or repair on the day.

Investigate and experiment at the beauty counters of
any department store. The consultants are very generous
with their advice, which is usually considerable and costs
you nothing. Or book a consultant, and discuss make-up
possibilities with her in the same way as you would for
your hair. Do you want her do your face on the day?

The bride's very own list

Wedding dress	*fittings and alterations completed on* ....
Flowers	*bouquet and hair decoration ordered*.............................
Gloves	*ordered*....................................
Shoes	*ordered*....................................
Make-up	*consultant booked*...................
Perfume	....
Hairdresser	*booked*.......................................
Headdress	*purchased* .... *delivered*...................................
Jewellery	....
Underwear	*purchase spare stockings*
Garter	*purchased*.................................

Choosing the groom's attire

DOES YOUR GROOM want to wear a gorgeous embroidered waistcoat, a scarlet cummerbund, gloves and a top hat on his wedding day? Whatever he has in mind he knows that he and his attendants will have to dress in matching outfits and in a manner that accords with the overall style of the wedding.

For a church wedding in which you plan to wear a traditional flowing white dress, the groom would be best dressed in the traditional morning suit with top hat and tails or a smart lounge suit. Any colours introduced should reflect the colours featured in your dress or the bridesmaids' dresses. For an informal registry office wedding he can choose a lounge suit that complements the style and colour of your outfit. It is not usual for the groom to wear a blazer and slacks at his wedding.

All the men in the party – the groom, the best man, the bride's father and the ushers – should be dressed alike. The groom may sport an embroidered waistcoat or coloured cummerbund, but if he's wearing a morning suit, so will the others. If he chooses a blue or grey lounge suit, the other men must choose the same colour although not necessarily of identical cut.

Morning suits are very expensive to buy and will rarely, if ever, be worn again, but they can be hired. The groom should take his best man and ushers with him to the fittings and to choose the accessories – shoes and socks should match the suit, and ties, handkerchieves and buttonholes should complement the general colour scheme.

Bookings for suits, as with most wedding arrangements, must be made well in advance – at least four months before the wedding. The best man is responsible for seeing to the delivery of the groom's outfit, and for returning it in good order after the wedding.

If worn, top hat and gloves should be removed by the groom and his party once inside the church. Both should then be carried at all times in the left hand – the hat by the brim. The groom should leave his hat and gloves in the pew when he reaches the chancel to be retrieved by the best man as the recessional starts.

The groom's wedding outfit

Morning suit	*chosen*...............................
	fittings...............................
Lounge suit	*purchased*...............................
Waistcoat	*purchased*...............................
Tie or bow tie	*purchased*...............................
Shirt	*purchased*...............................
Shoes and socks	*purchased*...............................

Arranging your honeymoon

ARRANGING YOUR HONEYMOON may seem more complicated than organising an ordinary holiday – partly because you're doing so much else at the same time – but in fact most of the key considerations are identical.

When you've booked your holiday, these are the things you need to do:

Inoculations: Check in good time whether you will need any inoculations for your holiday destination. Some injections can make you feel unwell, which is the last thing you need when you have so much else to do.

Special visas: Find out whether you need any special visas, and check that both your passports are valid.

Passports: Your honeymoon must be booked in the name stated in your passport. So, if you plan to travel under your married name, you need to apply at least three months in advance to the Passport Office to change the name in your passport. They will then send your passport to the minister or registrar to give to you after the marriage. If you do not change the name in your passport, remember to take the marriage certificate on honeymoon.

Insurance and currency: Make sure you have good and reasonable travel insurance, and don't forget to order and take travellers' cheques and foreign currency.

Packing: Make a list of all the things you need to take and pack your case well in advance. Use a separate small bag for your first night's gear. Some grooms whisk the bride off to a honeymoon at a secret location. If this is going to happen to you, make sure he tells you the type of location, so that you can pack appropriate clothing.

Care of documentation: Ask the groom to make sure the best man takes charge of the holiday documentation until after the reception.

Cutting costs

A honeymoon can make another big dent in your finances at a time when they are already stretched thin. Ways of cutting your honeymoon costs include: going for a shorter time than two weeks; staying with relatives or friends, or using their holiday homes; booking early or, alternatively, taking advantage of last-minute deals; self-catering; travelling out of season or mid-week. If your reception is to be held in a hotel, it may offer first-night discounts to the bride and groom.

You should also decide whether you will be taking your usual summer holiday during the year of your wedding. If you are, maybe you could limit yourself to a shorter honeymoon, or perhaps one closer to home. After all, whatever you do, it's bound to be memorable.

5

Countdown to the big day

❧

T HE BIG DECISIONS have all been taken long ago and all the arrangements are nearly complete, yet for many brides the week before the big day is filled with emotional tensions and fears that the arrangements will all go wrong.

The week before

Now is a good time to fine-tune the final arrangements, for example, finalising seating plans if you are having a sit-down meal, getting the place cards ready, setting aside an hour or so to try on your complete outfit – including the underwear. Above all, make sure that everyone involved knows as much as possible. The wedding rehearsal is the obvious time for this kind of conversation, but if there is no rehearsal, call a meeting.

Your aim should be to delegate everything successfully – so that the immediate families have nothing to worry about except getting themselves ready and getting to the church or registry office on time!

Other tasks and events of your final week as a single woman are as follows:

• *Contact your suppliers* – to confirm your orders, pay any necessary deposits, give them the final numbers (you probably won't know until now what they are), provide confirmation of the timings of the day, addresses, contact telephone numbers and any useful itineraries.

• *Attend rehearsal*. During the week before the church service, there is usually a full run through the ceremony with all the attendants present. This makes sure everyone knows the procedures for the day. You do not wear your wedding clothes for this practice run.

• *Present gifts to attendants.* You may like to give your attendants their gifts now. You and the groom can organise an informal supper or lunch party after the rehearsal when you can hand out the presents.

• *Make church seating plan.* If the church is a small one, it's a good idea to work out a seating plan – at least for the first few rows of relatives. Give the plan to the head usher at the rehearsal or at the meal afterwards so that there will be no confusion on the day.

Above all try to relax as much as possible during the week. Remember too that you are part of a team – and are not solely responsible for having to remember what everyone else should be doing. Everyone will be wishing you well and willing you to have a fabulous day.

The big day

E VEN IF YOU AND YOUR FIANCE are already living together, it is traditional that the bride and groom do not meet on the wedding day until he greets her at the altar, so many brides choose to return to the family home for their last night as a single woman. Your main duty as the bride is to get yourself ready in time. Do try to eat a good breakfast – you'll be on your feet for many hours today – and although you shouldn't see the groom there is no reason why you shouldn't ring him and offer him a few words of encouragement.

At your home
• 2 hours before – you make your final preparations with or without the help of a hairdresser and make-up artist and the chief bridesmaid, leaving time to spend a few minutes alone with your parents. Many brides choose to change their engagement ring over to their right hand before they leave the house. Your mother will then join the bridesmaids in the car, and you and your father follow on in another vehicle.

At the groom's home
• The best man assists the groom with his preparations.

At the church
• 40–50 minutes to go – ushers arrive to hand out

order of service sheets, buttonholes and direct the congregation to the pews. The bride's family and friends sit on the left (facing the altar); the groom's family and friends sit on the right. Close family members should sit in the first few rows.

• 30 minutes to go – minister, organist and bell-ringers arrive. Bell-ringing starts, and the organ plays quietly.

• 20 minutes to go – groom and best man arrive and pose for any photographs. The best man makes sure that he and the groom take their seats (in the front pew on the right of the centre aisle) a few minutes before you arrive.

• 20 minutes to go – chief bridesmaid, bridesmaids and flower girls arrive with your mother and wait in the church porch until you arrive with your father.

• 15 minutes to go – you and your father arrive by car. Photographs may be taken. Your mother or chief bridesmaid helps adjust your gown, train and veil. Double check that your engagement ring is on your right hand.

• 2 minutes to go – either the chief usher or a male member of your family escorts your mother to her seat in the front pew. Always the last guest to be seated, this is a signal for the congregation that the ceremony is about to begin. The organist begins to play the chosen processional music.

• 1 minute to go – ushers take their seats in pews at the rear. The groom and best man stand; bridesmaids and page boys line up behind you or form two columns at the main door and fall in behind you. If there is a flower girl, she stands in front of you, ready to walk in front of you scattering petals. The minister will greet you and then return to the altar to wait for the procession at the chancel steps (in which case the choir is already seated).

However, if there is to be a full choral service, the minister may greet you at the porch and then the procession will consist of the choir, followed by the minister, then the flower girl, you and your father, then the attendants in pairs (the youngest usually go first).

• Zero minutes – the bridal party enters the church and proceeds up the aisle, the groom and best man move from the front pew to the chancel steps, with the best man at the groom's right, standing a pace behind him. All the congregation stand.

At the chancel steps, you are taken by your father to stand at the groom's left. Your father then moves to stand to your left and a pace behind you. The bridal attendants remain in the aisle behind you. Either you lift your veil yourself or the chief bridesmaid will do it for you and she takes your bouquet and gloves (if you are wearing any). She holds these items throughout the service until after the register has been signed.

The order of service

The service, which will last for about 30 minutes, begins with the minister greeting the congregation. Depending on the church, the precise order and type of service varies but usually opens with:
• a hymn
• a prayer or Bible reading
• an address from the minister

Your father takes your right hand and gives it to the minister who passes it to the groom. You then make your vows. The best man places the rings on the face of the prayer book which he then gives to the minister. Your husband fits your ring onto the third finger of your left hand, then you place his ring on the same finger on his hand. Then you kiss each other.

The minister then gives the blessing, some prayers may follow while you and the groom kneel at the chancel steps. There may be another hymn, and if Holy Communion or a Nuptial Mass is part of the service, it will take place at this point.

The recessional

Taking your husband's left arm, you leave the chancel after the minister. The minister leads the bridal couple, their parents, the best man and bridesmaid into the vestry to sign the register and certificate. The best man carries the groom's and his own gloves and hat.

Signing the register

The marriage register and certificate will be ready to sign. While music is played in the church or perhaps an anthem is sung, the register is signed by the minister, yourself (using your maiden name for the last time, if you intend to take your husband's surname), the groom and two adult witnesses – usually the two fathers or the best man and chief bridesmaid (if she is over 18). However, there is no reason why both mothers or a representative from each family cannot sign. Once the register is signed you and the groom are legally married.

The minister then hands the certificate to the groom. A few photographs may be taken. Then you are given your bouquet by the chief bridesmaid and the groom offers you his left arm – having taken his hat and gloves from the best man. As the music changes and the bells ring out, the bridal party – the bridesmaids carrying the train, if necessary – walk back down the aisle. Your mother and his father, followed by his mother and your father walk behind and they are followd by relatives from the front pews and then the congregation comes after them.

After the service

When the wedding party and congregation emerge from the church, they can start to relax. Confetti and rice may be thrown – if this is allowed – and the best man will start to organise those guests and family members who are to be included in the formal wedding photographs.

The best man will also let everyone know when it is time to leave for the reception and escort you and the groom to the first waiting car. Wedding protocol demands the second car for the bride's mother and groom's father and the third is for the bride's father and groom's mother. The attendants may follow in their car, or they may share a car with either pair of parents.

All the guests then make their way to the reception; the best man is usually the last to leave the church as he checks for left belongings and ensures that every guest has the means to travel, although he must also make sure he arrives as early as possible at the reception!

At the registry office

A civil ceremony is shorter and much less formal than a church wedding. Although licensed venues can sometimes take a large number of guests, few registry offices are very big and most civil weddings are restricted to close family and a few friends. .

As registry offices are busy places, try to avoid arriving either too early or too late as you may get caught up in another wedding. The registrar may want to have a brief word with both of you before the ceremony, to check that everything is in order, in which case your guests can take their seats. The whole ceremony will last around 10 to 15 minutes and must not contain any religious elements, although you can ask whether you can include some music and/or poems to make the service more personal.

Couples wishing to have the ceremony videoed or photographs taken, must ask the permission of the registrar. After you have been married, you and the groom, the two witnesses and the registrar all sign the marriage certificate.

Once the marriage has taken place and the required signatures have been given, you and the groom and your guests will normally leave the registry office, perhaps stopping for a few photographs outside, and go on to the reception. If you marry in a licensed venue, you usually move into another room for the reception.

At the reception

ALTHOUGH NOT THE FIRST to leave the church, your parents (as host and hostess of the reception) need to arrive at the reception venue first. At a very formal reception, the guests are usually welcomed by a receiving line and a toastmaster may announce the guests as they approach it. Essentially, the receiving line allows each guest to meet all the wedding party and give their congratulations. The usual order for a full receiving line is :

- Bride's mother
- Bride's father
- Groom's mother
- Groom's father
- Bride
- Groom
- Best man
- Chief bridesmaid
- Other attendants

Each guest arriving is then introduced to each subsequent member of the party. Nowadays receiving lines tend to be far faster moving than in days gone by. At the end of the line make sure each guest is served a drink or an aperitif. Wine, or, if finances allow, champagne or buck's fizz (orange juice and champagne) is a good choice. However, if you don't feel like it, the receiving line needn't be formal – the families can simply gather in a group to welcome guests when they arrive.

Seating the guests

At a formal reception with a sit-down meal, the toast-master will ask the guests to take their seats at the pre-arranged time. At an informal affair the best man will ask the bride and groom to take their seats. The order in which the rest of the wedding party and guests proceed into the dining room is as follows:

- Bride's father with groom's mother
- Bride's mother with groom's father
- Best man with chief bridesmaid
- Other attendants
- Ushers
- Guests

The ushers and best man should help the guests find their places on the seating plan and help them take their places. If there is a minister of religion present he should be asked to say grace. If the reception is a buffet, make it clear to the guests whether they should collect their first course before taking their seats, or sit down at their places and go to the serving tables a few at a time when invited.

Speeches and toasts

At a sit-down meal, the speeches and toasts usually take place after the meal, before the cake is cut. At a buffet, the speeches are usually made after the cake is cut. The toast-master usually presides over the ceremony but if there is no toastmaster present, the best man will stand and ask for silence before introducing the first speaker. In the past, it was quite common for the bride to welcome her guests – and if you wish to do so, a good time to do it would be immediately before the traditional speeches. The customary order of speeches is:

• Bride's father, who ends by proposing a toast to the health of the bride and groom.

• Groom, who responds on behalf of the bride and himself and ends by toasting the bridesmaids.

• Best man, who replies on behalf of the bridesmaids and reads the telegrams as well as giving a speech.

Do ask the speakers to keep their speeches reasonably short – no wedding speech should last for more than 10 minutes each, 15 minutes at the maximum. It's important to make sure all the guests have a charged glass for the toasts. Everyone stands to drink the toasts.

The cake-cutting ceremony usually comes next, you and the groom cutting the first slice together before the caterers take it away to be cut for the guests. This is often the signal for the guests to leave the table to mingle.

Dancing

If there is dancing – whether to a disco or a band – it tends to start after the cake cutting. The bride and groom always start the proceedings with a slow dance. After a few minutes the best man and chief bridesmaid join in, followed by the parents of the couple. Guests do not join in until the second dance. You should then dance with all the members of the wedding party and close family members of the opposite sex. The best man dances with all the ladies of the wedding party, including yourself, and with as many guests as possible. He also takes care of you and the groom, ensuring that you talk to all your guests.

Grand exit

The best man should remind you both when it is time to change for your departure and give you the tickets and documentation you need for your honeymoon. You retire with the chief bridesmaid to change into your going-away outfit, as does the groom, accompanied by the best man.

Before you both leave – possibly to drive away in a specially decorated car with boots and foam inscriptions – you should make a tour of the room, thanking guests and especially your parents. Either the best man or the bride's father will announce your imminent departure.

The groom may present his mother and mother-in-law with bouquets, and the bride always throws her bouquet over her shoulder towards the assembled female guests. According to tradition, the one who catches the bouquet can expect to be the next bride. The guests should never depart before the bride and groom but most start to drift away soon after the couple have left.

Many couples choose to spend the first night at a hotel close to the reception, if only to gather their strength again after the big day. Most, if not all, couples will be absolutely exhausted so splash out on the most comfortable hotel you can afford and relax in style. Arrange a late breakfast in bed next morning and don't aim to start travelling to your honeymoon destination until early afternoon.

After the wedding

ALTHOUGH THE WEDDING DAY celebrations are officially over when the newlyweds leave the reception, a number of tasks need to be carried out during the honeymoon:

• *Clothing* – the best man and chief bridesmaid return any hired attire, and keep any deposits, plus receipts for cleaning for the return of the couple.

• *Photographs/videos* – the bride's mother deals with orders for photographs.

• *Cake* – the bride's mother sends small pieces of wedding cake to those who were unable to attend the wedding day celebrations.

• *Press reports* – many couples arrange for a report of the wedding to appear in the local paper. The bride's mother is responsible for buying and saving copies.

Post-honeymoon

You may have aleady written your thank-you notes for gifts that arrived before the wedding, but there are bound to be notes to be sent for presents that arrived on the day. It's also a thoughtful gesture to send both sets of parents, and all the attendants, a handwritten letter, thanking them for all their help and support on the wedding day.

Remember also the following:
• *Will* – as marriage automatically invalidates any pre-

vious wills, it is important to make new provisions. If you have not made one before it is important that you do so now there are two of you to consider.

• *Pension* – if not involved in your company's pension scheme, it is a good idea to take out a savings plan.

• *Home contents insurance* – the value of your joint possessions should be assessed (the wedding list can be helpful here) or reassessed, if you were living together before you were married, and insurance taken out.

Tradition has it that the new couple should entertain both sets of parents within the first three months of the wedding, followed by the best man, together with bridesmaids and ushers, at the new home. You may also like to consider holding a dinner party for those who were unable to attend the wedding and perhaps also invite people who gave a gift, even though they weren't invited.

A change of name

There is no legal requirement for the bride to change her surname when she marries. If you wish to continue to use your maiden name there is no need to change any documents. Some brides decide to use both – the maiden name for professional purposes and the married name socially. If you do decide to change your surname, you should inform your employer, bank, building society, insurance companies, credit-card companies, passport office, Inland Revenue, DSS, DVLC, GP, dentist and so on in writing.

6

Wedding Diary

❦

Nine to Six Month Countdown

1. *Discuss plans with your families*

2. *Set the budget*

3. *Choose the type of service and size of reception*

4. *Set a date and, as soon as possible, book the church, or registry office. You and the groom must sort out legal requirements and present documents to the marriage officer or priest*

5. *Choose your attendants, and ask the groom to select his bestman and ushers*

6. *Meet your mother and the groom's mother to discuss wedding guests*

7. *Florist and photographer must be booked now –some have full diaries for the next year*

8. *Discuss transport with the groom, and hire the wedding cars. Many of these companies are, like the florist and photographer, booked a year ahead*

9. Book caterer and the drinks supplier

10. Hire of catering equipment if necessary

11. You and the groom should discuss the music you want for the church and the reception, and the musicians must be booked as soon as possible. It may help to talk to the priest about choirs and a soloist for the service

12. The groom might be planning a secret destination for the honeymoon, but it must be booked and your passports need to be checked. And find out if you need any immunisation injections. If you want your passport in your married name approach the Passport Office for information

13. Book time off work

14. Draw up a wedding list and either pick the stores where you are going to leave the list, or give a copy to your mother

15. Prepare your invitation list and consult a printer

16. Choose a wedding dress and meet your bridesmaids to discuss their clothes with them

17. Buy the underwear you intend to wear on your wedding day

Three Month Countdown

1. If you are having your dress made, or any alterations are required, check your fitting dates with the dressmaker

2. Discuss flowers with florist and finalise your choice of colours and blooms

3. Order your cake

4. Select your going-away outfit, and listen carefully to your chief bridesmaid. She may be trying to give you hints about the right clothes to pack for the secret destination honeymoon

5. Have all the necessary deposits been made? No supplier will do anything on the strength of a verbal quotation. Written agreements and deposits will ensure their services

6. Do all suppliers have the itinerary and venues for the day? Do they have your contact telephone numbers and addresses? Do you have theirs?

7. Collect stationery and send out wedding invitations

8. Choose – and wrap – gifts for the groom, attendants and the mothers. This takes longer than aniticipated, and if the task is delayed at all the giving of presents becomes an anxiety instead of a pleasure

9. Have you made any change in guest numbers? Does this mean a change in the size of the marquee? Are any extra costs involved? If so, confirm in writing

10. Check that there are adequate access and parking facilities for florists', caterers' and the marquee's trucks

11. Review your budget with your groom and both sets of parents

12. Choose your wedding rings

13. If you are changing your name notify your bank, doctor, dentist and so on. Also tell them if you are changing your address

One Month Before

1. *Catch up on thank you notes for presents received*

2. *Confirm the number of guests expected with the caterer so that there are the right numbers of chairs, tables, equipment and staff—and, of course, that there will be enough food*
   Is the caterer feeding the musicians? If so what arrangements have been made for them, and what will it cost?

3. *Confirm that the florist knows where and when to deliver bouquets, posies and buttonholes*
   Have you ensured that the florist will return to the reception venue to tidy up, and collect pedestals and baskets? When are they able to do this?

4. *Send the photographer a comprehensive list of the pictures you want taken. Will he or she work at the church and the reception?*
   If not, consider arranging for someone else to take photographs until the last guest leaves

5. *Confirm that the caterer, mother or bridesmaid will take the cake to the reception and assemble it*
   Organise the cakestand and a knife, and someone to decorate the stand. This may be your mother or a caterer, or even your bridesmaid

6.   Give the musicians a list of your favourite tunes. Can people dance to the music they will be playing?

Arrange a room where the entertainers can change, and leave their possessions somewhere secure

7.   Organise for rubbish removal and security at the reception.

8.   Finalise your seating plan

9.   Send the car hire firm a written itinerary

One Week Before

1. *Make sure all the wedding party know their various duties*

2. *Have a night out with your girlfriends*

3. *Practise your make-up one more time*

4. *Check that bestman knows times to collect button-holes and service sheets; that he has your passports, travel documents and wedding rings. He will organize the ushers and the fleet of wedding cars. He sould have money for marriage fees and emergencies*

Eve of The Wedding

This could be a day of panic, but it can – and should be – a day of whimsy, nostalgia, dreaminess and excitement.

You should wake up confident that everything is in place for the big day. Reassure yourself with a phone call to your bridesmaid to ensure times, and check with the best man that, yes, he will pick up the buttonholes and he does know what time to take the groom to the church. If you still feel panicky, you could check with the florist, the chauffuer, the photographer and the caterer that they, too, are fully prepared for the next day.

There is a checklist for you on the next page.

Now take it easy. Enjoy your manicure and pedicure, and meet your mother or godmother or granny, or all three for lunch. Give or deliver your gifts to your parents and your attendants if you havn't yet done so. Lay out all the beautiful things you are going to wear the next day, and have a quiet supper and get to bed early.

Last Minute Advice

1. Check times with bridesmaid

2. Remind bestman of buttonholes

3. Check times and delivery of bouquets and buttonholes with florist

4. Check times with chauffeur

5. Check appointment with hairdresser

6. Make sure your going-away outfit is pressed and bagged. Ask the best man to collect the honeymoon luggage, and deliver it to the reception venue

On the Day

You are not going to spend your morning worrying and

ticking off yet another checklist.

Have a perfect wedding

Legal and Religious Information Centres

You may need help with the religious and legal rules regarding marriage, particularly if you and the groom belong to different churches. Perhaps you come from different faiths, or one of you has been married before. Here is a list of numbers where you can seek advice:

Church of England Enquiry Centre	- 0171–222 9011
Episcopal Church of Scotland	- 0131–225 6357
Church of Scotland Office	- 0131–225 5722
Marriage Care (Formerly Catholic Marriage Advisory Council)	- 0171–243 1898
Methodist Press and Information Centre	- 0171–222 8010
Baptist Union	- 01235–517700
United Reform Church	- 0171–916 2020
Greek Orthodox Church Information	- 0171–723 4787
Jewish Marriage Council	- 0181–203 6311
Muslim Information Centre/Services	- 0171–272 5170
The Hindu Sociey	- 0181–534 8879

If you want information on the requirements for a civil wedding, call:

Register General for England and Wales	- 0151–471 4200
General Register Office for Scotland	- 0131–334 0380
General Register Office for Northern Ireland	- 01232–250000
Register General, Dublin	- 00 3531–6711000